Lights for the Night

A First Look at Illumination

BY SOLVEIG PAULSON RUSSELL

ILLUSTRATED BY PATRICIA FRANK KORBET

HENRY Z. WALCK, INC.   NEW YORK

621.32   Russell, Solveig Paulson
  R   Lights for the night; a first look
         at illumination; illus. by Patricia
         Frank Korbet.   Walck, 1970
             47p. illus.

             A clear text showing man's progress
         from use of torches to atomic-
         powered electricity.

             1. Lighting   I. Illus.   II. Title

TEXT COPYRIGHT © 1970 BY SOLVEIG PAULSON RUSSELL. ILLUSTRATIONS COPYRIGHT © 1970
BY PATRICIA FRANK KORBET. ALL RIGHTS RESERVED. ISBN: 0-8098-1170-7. LIBRARY OF
CONGRESS CATALOG CARD NUMBER: 72-119572. PRINTED IN THE UNITED STATES OF AMERICA.

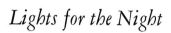

Lights for the Night

To Ann Marie Prengamon's children

FIRST LIGHT

Long ago, when the first people lived on earth, the only light they saw at night came from the moon and the stars. They had no lamps, no light of any kind, other than moonlight and starlight.

When the sun went down, women and children could not see well enough to find berries to eat. Men could not fish or hunt. There was little to do except wait for the sunlight of another day.

Nobody knows when or how the cavemen first learned to control fire. Perhaps lightning struck a dead tree and someone discovered that when he added wood to the blaze, the fire kept on burning. Fire made brightness, and if they protected the flames and kept them burning, they could have nighttime light. The burning wood gave them warmth and light to see each other, and it kept away the wild animals. When, by some lucky accident, the cave people's raw meat got so close to fire that it cooked, they learned that the taste of food changed with heating. They liked the change, and so cooking began.

By moving burning embers or flaming sticks inside their caves, they brought light and warmth into their homes. It was easier, too, to keep the fire going in the shelter of the cave.

The caveman saw that his stone hammer sometimes set off tiny sparks when he struck it on his flint tools. If the sparks landed in dry leaves or grass, a fire would start. Rubbing a hard stick against soft wood would also make sparks. If he could catch the sparks in some dry material, he could have his own fire.

TORCHES

Then someone saw that if he pulled a long stick of wood, that was burning at only one end, from the bonfire, he could carry light. He had a torch. He could walk in the darkness in a circle of light from a burning stick.

Men learned that if the stick were dipped in animal fat or in the pitch that oozed from trees, the light was brighter and lasted longer. And if the fat or pitch was wrapped tightly with plant fibers at the end of the torch, it would last still longer.

Torches were useful for moving about at night, and they could be fastened to walls for inside light. But they were dangerous, and needed to be watched, because sparks and burning pitch dropped from them. Torches were used from early times up to and through the Middle Ages.

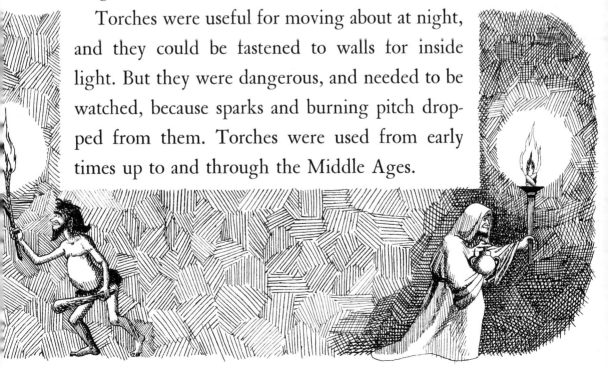

FIRST LAMPS

Perhaps one day in those faraway times of the Stone Age a glowing ember from a bonfire or torch fell into a discarded animal's skull that had some fat left in it. The fat began to melt and to burn. Somebody saw that only the fat burned, not the skull. The skull was just a container for the burning fat. It was a lamp.

So men learned that fat, in a container, would burn to give light. Then they hunted for flat stones with hollows in them to fill with fat and oil. They also put fat into empty shells. When the fat was lit from live embers, men had made improvements in lighting. They had the first lamps—fifteen thousand or more years ago.

WICKS

As time passed people learned many things about controlling fire. One thing they learned was that a rush, or a reed, from a pond could be used to make a better lamp.

The center, or pith, of a reed is not solid. It has layers and layers of little air pockets, or hair-like tubes, in it. When the reed, or anything with little spaces in it is put into liquid, the liquid moves up, from one space to another.

When a reed was put into a container of oil and lit at its end the reed did not burn away quickly. A clean, steady flame burned only at the tip of the reed, where the oil continued to be drawn into it from the container. The reed was a wick.

Many years later, when men had advanced to using cotton for weaving cloth, small bits of cotton and cloth, which have air tubes between the threads, were used for wicks, too. These were placed in the lamps with their points out over the lamp edges. Sometimes to get a brighter light, people used a number of wicks in one lamp.

IMPROVED LAMPS

Thousands of years before Christ, people learned to make containers of baked clay and of metal, and they used these for their lamps. Over the centuries they developed containers that would not spill oil as easily as the saucerlike first lamps. Lamps were made deeper. Some had handles, like many of the gravy dishes of today, so they were easier to move. Some had lids. There were holes or spouts in some of them for the wicks to come through. A few were made beautiful by artists who took pleasure in shaping them.

In different parts of the world men used whatever fats or oils they could find for their lamps. Fats and oils from wild and tame animals, from fish, and from olives and nuts were used for many hundreds of years in different parts of the world. But whale oil, when it was brought in by whaling ships in the eighteenth century, was considered to be the best lamp oil by many people for a long time. It was used to brighten the dark corners of many of the homes in our country until about a hundred years ago.

CANDLES

Lamps could use only oils or fats that melted easily. Solid fats, such as tallow from mutton or the fat of beef, could not be used in lamps. Beeswax was also too hard to be used. These fats, though, could be used for candles. A candle's flame melts the wax or hard fat around the wick and burns it. If you look at a burning candle, you will see the little pool of liquid, or melted wax, that circles the wick.

The Romans were probably the earliest people to make candles. They used beeswax. The very first candles, we think, had the pith of a reed for a wick. To make the candle, the reed was peeled, leaving only the center pith. Then the piece of pith was carefully dipped into melted beeswax.

When it was covered with wax, the pith was held up until the coating of wax hardened. When the wax was hard it was dipped again and again. As the wax hardened after each dipping the candle became bigger and bigger.

Beeswax candles were expensive, since beeswax was hard to get. These candles were used mostly in temples and churches. Tallow was easier to get. Because of this many people could make and use tallow candles in their homes.

It was hard to prepare candle wicks from reeds. Then it was discovered that cotton string wicks could be used. But cotton wicks were not straight and stiff as reeds were, and they needed to be straight for dipping. So people tied small weights to the ends of the cotton string wicks, so that they would stay straight up and down as they were dipped. When the candle was big enough, the weights were cut off.

It took a long time to dip each candle; and many candles were needed. So people thought up ways of making several candles at once. They tied a number of wicks with weights on them to a rod. They could dip all the wicks together, or they could pour melted fat over all the wicks, catching the unused fat in a dish. When the first layer hardened they dipped, or poured, and hardened again, and again and again.

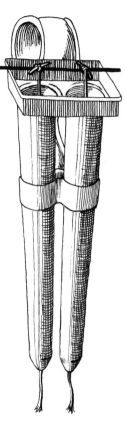

The next improvement in candle making was the use of candle molds. A hundred and fifty years ago candle molds were used in most American homes. They were usually made of tin and looked like a row of little tin pipes, standing on end and fastened together. Each pipe had a hole in the bottom for the wick to go through.

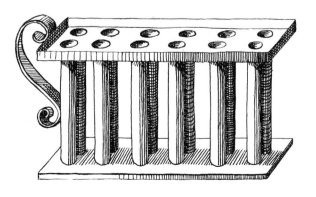

A cotton wick was threaded through the bottom hole of each pipe and tied across a rod placed at the top of the molds. Then melted tallow was poured into the molds. When it cooled and hardened around the wicks, the candles could be lifted from the molds, ready to be used in a candle holder, or a candlestick.

Some candle holders had spikes sticking up in the base. The candle end was pushed down over the spike to hold the candle erect. Other candle holders had cups or bands of metal into which the ends of the candles fitted. Some candle sticks were plain, others were beautifully made, just as they are today.

People also used rushlights for light. Rush-lights were made from the pith of reeds dipped in candle material, usually tallow, but sometimes beeswax. When used outside, people held the slender rushlights; but in homes they were placed in holders. Rushlights burned away within an hour's time. If they had been dipped many times they would have become candles.

So candles, which melt wax or hard fat and burn it away slowly, came into common use. The people who first came to our country depended on them for afterdark comfort, along with oil lamps and the firelight from fireplaces. Today, we too, still use candles for special occasions.

Candles provided people with a light that was easier to control than a torch, which often dropped hot coals or pitch. But they couldn't just go walking along with a lighted candle in their hands. The smallest breeze would soon have caused the yellow flame to go out. A protective chimney of some kind placed around the flame to shield it worked well. With these, men had lanterns.

Thin layers of animal horns were used as chimneys for the first lanterns. Placed around the light in frames, they kept the wind from the flame, and allowed the light to gleam through. Later lanterns were made of tin or brass, or other metal. They were cages with small holes or openings in the sides to let the light shine out. Some of them were beautiful, but none of the early lanterns gave a great deal of light.

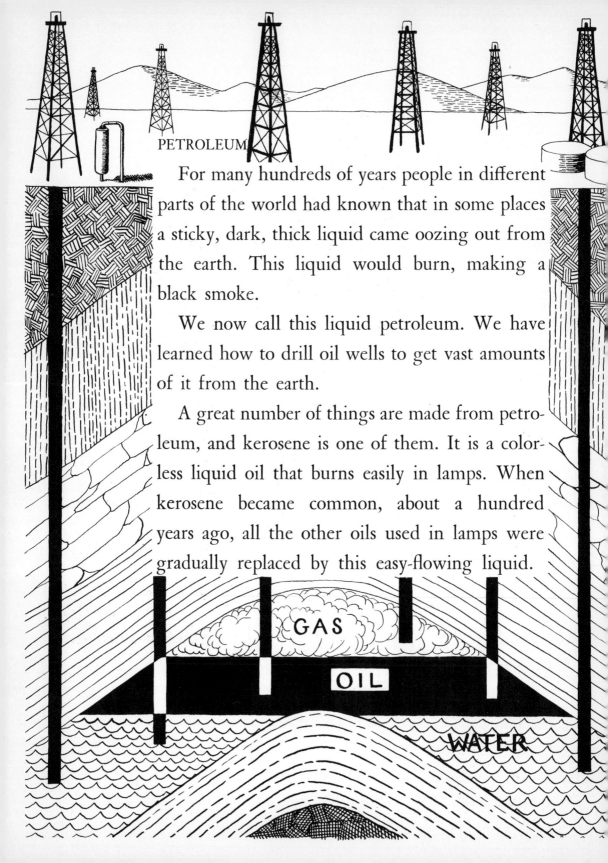

PETROLEUM

For many hundreds of years people in different parts of the world had known that in some places a sticky, dark, thick liquid came oozing out from the earth. This liquid would burn, making a black smoke.

We now call this liquid petroleum. We have learned how to drill oil wells to get vast amounts of it from the earth.

A great number of things are made from petroleum, and kerosene is one of them. It is a colorless liquid oil that burns easily in lamps. When kerosene became common, about a hundred years ago, all the other oils used in lamps were gradually replaced by this easy-flowing liquid.

GAS

OIL

WATER

Until a little less than two hundred years ago, wicks for lamps were just placed in containers of oil. All of these lamps were smoky. Then a man named Argand, who lived in Switzerland, discovered that wicks smoked because, lying in oil, they didn't have enough exposure to air.

After much study Argand made a new kind of wick. It was woven in a tube shape, like a tiny stocking leg. He made two brass tubes, one a little larger than the other. He put the smaller tube inside the wick and then pushed the larger tube over it. The wick was held in an upright position between the two metal tubes. Then he pulled the wick so that a little of it was above the tubes. Most of the wick stuck out at the bottom of the tubes into the oil of the lamp. It burned with a clear, bright flame, since air could reach both the inside and outside of the wick.

GLASS CHIMNEYS

After Argand's wick proved so successful, other wicks were made and placed in metal burners. Some were flat, others round.

Then, in the first part of the eighteenth century, glass chimneys were made for the burners. These kept the breezes away from the flame so that it burned brighter and did not flicker. Some lamps also had fancy shades of glass or pottery to make them beautiful and to soften the light.

Kerosene lamps and lanterns, too, with glass chimneys, have been used for a long time. They are still used where there is no electricity, or at times when electricity fails.

GAS FOR LIGHT

Gas lights were developed when scientists learned that when coal is heated, gases are released from it. Gas cannot be seen, but if a lighted match is placed near gas, it immediately bursts into flame. Gas can be collected by heating coal in great ovens. It can be stored in tanks and piped to the homes of people who use it.

Gas was first used for lighting about two hundred years ago. At first it was burned from the ends of tubes in a single flame. Then someone closed the end of the tube and made three little holes in the closed end so that less gas would come out at a time. The light from the three holes was brighter than that from the single flame. When a row of small holes was made, the light was still better. A flow of gas through burners with many little holes not only gives better light, but also uses less gas.

IMPROVEMENTS IN GAS LIGHTS—MANTLES

Just as a better wick and burner improved the kerosene lamp, so mantles improved gas lamps.

Mantles are like little knitted sacks that are fastened at the end of a gas burner. They are made of knitted cotton material that is treated with metallic chemicals. They are fastened to the gas burner before the gas is turned on. Then the mantles are lit by a match. The flame from the match burns away the knitted material and leaves a fragile sack of metal ashes hanging to the burner.

The sack is full of tiny holes left from the burning away of the knitted threads. When the gas is turned on and lit, the little sack fills out.

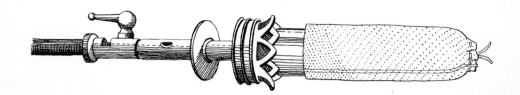

The burning gas makes it white hot, and it gives a bright white light. Gas mantles are easily broken after they become ash, but with care many are used for a surprisingly long time.

The mantles of metallic ash give off light because they do not burn away when heated, but instead glow with brilliance. Light made from the heating of unburnable material is called incandescent light.

Mantles were invented in 1885 by an Australian scientist named Welsbach. Many people in the world who use gas lights and lanterns have benefited from his work.

NATURAL GAS

Gas doesn't always have to be made. There are large amounts of natural gas in our earth. Sometimes it is found when men drill oil wells.

Natural gas springs, or places where gas comes out of the ground, were known to people of ancient times. When these springs were lighted by a live ember people were filled with wonder. They were probably afraid, too, for they did not understand where the flame came from.

Now natural gas is stored in tanks and piped to millions of people to use in heating and cooking.

ELECTRIC LIGHT

When the earliest people were using torches and bonfires for light, the strange force we call electricity existed. The cave dwellers saw the lightning flash in the sky, but they did not know the flash was electricity. Through all the years when smoky fat and oil burned in crude lamps, during the years the pioneers burned candles, electricity was waiting to be used.

Electricity is a form of energy. We cannot see it as we see oil, but we can see what it does.

It took long years of study and many experiments before men first learned how to explain electricity, how to control it, and how to conduct it along a wire.

It is only in the last hundred years that electricity has come into use. Before then all the lights people had were made by burning something.

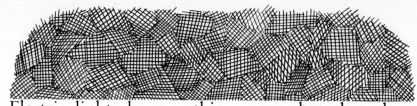

Electric lights burn nothing away, but they do come from electric heat.

The energy of electricity makes heat when it is forced to flow in regulated ways through material such as some kind of metal wire. Copper wire is most commonly used in electrical wiring.

The first electric light was an arc light. It was made in England about 1808 by Sir Humphry Davy. Davy connected electric wires to two carbon rods. The rods were pointed toward each other with a small space between the points. When the electricity was turned on, it jumped from one carbon rod to the other, heating the points white hot and giving a brilliant light in an arc, or arch shape. But the carbon soon burned away and then the bright white light went out.

Arc lights were not really successful until 1876. Then Charles Francis Brush of Ohio invented a way of holding carbon rods in place and at

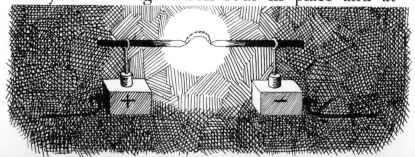

the same time pushing them together as fast as the ends burned away.

Arc lights were not satisfactory for home use. They were rather dirty, and the carbon rods had to be replaced when they were burned away. But they were good lights for outside use.

In searching for a better electric light, inventors saw that they needed some kind of thread or wire that could be heated white hot and which would not quickly burn away. Such a thread, or wire, was called a filament.

To keep the filament from burning away, it had to be placed in a glass globe from which all air was pumped. There also had to be a way of connecting the filament with electric wires.

Joseph Wilson Swan made the first hot filament in England in 1876. But his lamp filament was made of carbon thread and it could not stand

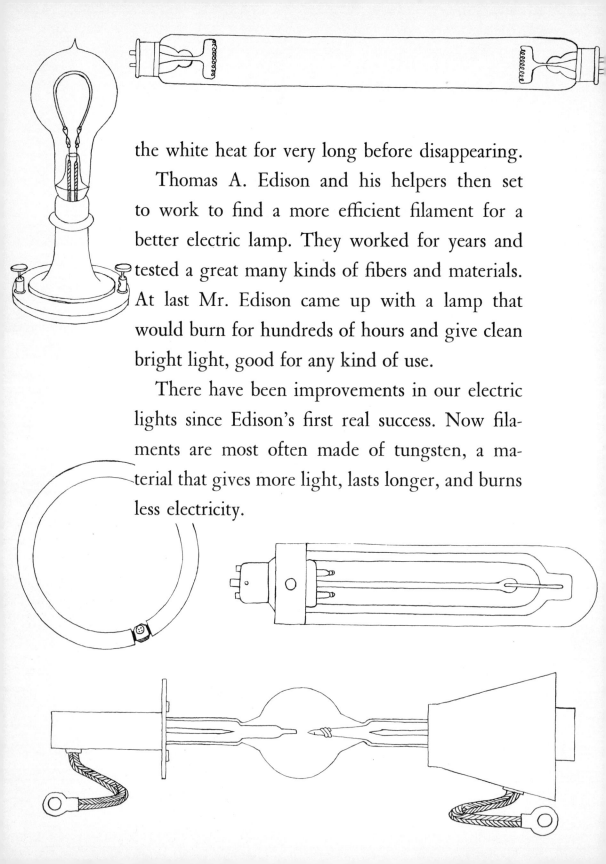

the white heat for very long before disappearing.

Thomas A. Edison and his helpers then set to work to find a more efficient filament for a better electric lamp. They worked for years and tested a great many kinds of fibers and materials. At last Mr. Edison came up with a lamp that would burn for hundreds of hours and give clean bright light, good for any kind of use.

There have been improvements in our electric lights since Edison's first real success. Now filaments are most often made of tungsten, a material that gives more light, lasts longer, and burns less electricity.

Now there are many kinds of electric lights. Neon, mercury vapor, and fluorescent lights are some of them. There are electric lights of many sizes for many uses. There will doubtless be others as time passes.

Electricity used by man is produced by electric generators. These are machines that have turning parts called turbines. As the turbines spin they produce the electric current that supplies the electricity we use.

The most common ways of making turbines spin are by using falling water from dams or waterfalls, or by using steam for power. Electricity can also be made from atomic energy. In the future the energy of atoms will probably be widely used for making electricity.

Today we can light our homes, streets, factories, ball parks, and other places in the night so that people can see as well as they can see in daylight. We have come a long way from the times when candle making required many hours of hard work to produce less light than we now have in a moment by flicking a light switch. Today whole cities may be lighted at once by a single person closing a switch that sends electricity instantly through miles of wires.

STREET LIGHTS

The Chinese used to hang lanterns at the entrances of their homes. Others in both Europe and America did this in early times, too. In some towns of England the people were required by law to hang a lantern at the door so that the street in front of the houses would be lighted. These were the first city street lights.

Lanterns beside doors were replaced by oil and kerosene lamps that were placed on posts along the streets. Then men had to be hired to take care of them. Each evening the "lamplighters" moved through the streets, carrying ladders so they could reach the lamps to light them. The next morning the lamplighters came again to blow out the lights, clean the lamps, and fill them with oil so that they would be ready for the next night.

When gas took the place of oil for street lamps, the lamplighters had to turn the gas on and light it in the evening, and turn it off when morning came. But when gas became very cheap the gas lights were often left to burn all through the day as well as at night. This was cheaper than hiring lamplighters to turn them on and off.

Now our streets are lighted by electric lights which shine out at night, lighting the way with more brightness than the torchcarriers of ancient times could ever have dreamed possible.

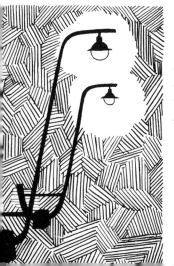

LIGHTHOUSES

Many years before Christ was born Egyptians had burning lights to guide sailors along rocky shores. The Egyptians built towers near the water's edge. From the tops of the towers they hung out metal baskets of blazing fuel.

Later the Romans built very high strong towers with flat tops. Fires were kept blazing on the tops of these towers to warn sailors at night. Signal fires such as these were used for many years.

Then, when oil lamps were developed, they were used in lighthouses built close to shore or on islands near the shore. Oil or gas is still used in some places, but for the most part the lighthouses of the world now use electricity.

There are glass-enclosed rooms at the top of lighthouses. From these rooms the powerful beams of light shine out for many miles over the sea. Special large lenses or reflectors surround the lights to increase their brightness. Many lights are made so that they turn slowly by machine. As they turn, they blink on and off at regular intervals. Sailors recognize the different lights by their way of flashing.

Lighthouse keepers, who usually live in or near the lighthouses, tend the lights. In the days of the early lighthouses they had to work hard to keep the light in good order. Now the job is much easier because of our improved ways of lighting. Some of our lighthouses are turned on or off by the use of automatic clocks or other devices.

In some dangerous places where lighthouses cannot be easily built lightships have been used, but with improved engineering and construction, their days are almost ended. These ships are anchored out at sea. Their light is placed at the top of a mast or on a frame built to hold it. A crew of men must always be on the lightship to take care of it and its light. Other boats bring food and supplies to the lightship and take the men to and from land when necessary.

Floating light buoys have small lights fastened to bases that float. They are anchored; and may be lighted by gas stored in tanks, by oil, or by electric batteries. Buoys are used to mark the channels or dangerous places for ocean travel.

ANIMAL LIGHT

There is one kind of light about which men are still asking questions. It is animal light.

Scientists have been trying for a long time to understand the cold light made by fireflies and some other insects. It is produced, we believe, by chemicals in the insects' bodies.

The Chinese and Japanese, and some other people, have made firefly lanterns by putting the insects into cages where their twinkling lights make a pretty sight.

Some very large beetles of Central America were used by Indians and early Spanish explorers for light. The Indians fastened them to their toes when they walked at night. Indian women put them in their hair for decorations. These big beetles give off enough light, it is said, for a few to light a room fairly well.

Deep in the sea, hundreds of feet below the surface, animal light glows too. Some fish, such as the black sea devil, produce phosphorescent light from parts of their bodies. Their light attracts other fish, which the sea devils then eat.

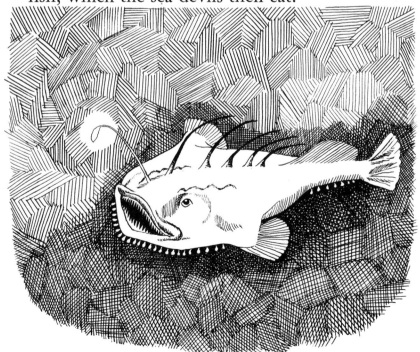

People have learned much since the earliest men had only fire to push away the darkness. But there is still much to be learned. As time passes and people extend their understanding, the day may come when the best lights of today may seem as ineffective as a burning torch does now.